today was completed in 1905. It was designed by Sir Aston (who also designed the Victoria and Albert Museum). It was at Dartmouth in 1938 that Queen Elizabeth II first laid eyes on Prince Philip at that year's passing out parade.

The only way to see Dartmouth is on foot. There is a car park in the centre with an example of Newcomen's steam atmospheric engine next to the Tourist Information Centre, but this soon fills up in the summer months, when a park and ride facility operates from the top of the town.

Bayards Fort, built in 1510 by Henry VIII to defend the town, stands at the end of Bayards Cove. Later from Bayards Cove the pilgrim fathers set sail for America, in the *Mayflower* and *Speedwell* in August 1620, but they returned to Plymouth after travelling some 300 miles because the ships were unseaworthy. Only the *Mayflower* then went ahead to complete this remarkable journey which is commemorated with a plaque. The cobbled quay has been a popular setting for makers of films and TV series, including 'The Onedin Line', with its Custom House that dates back to 1662.

Dartmouth from a watercolour by Frank H. Mason R I

1147–90 Fleets for the 2nd and 3rd Crusades assembled and sailed from the Estuary.

1347 Dartmouth sent only 31 ships fewer than Fowey (Cornwall) and Yarmouth (Norfolk) to besiege Calais. At this time Dartmouth was the fourth richest town in Devon after Exeter, Plymouth and Barnstaple.

1377 & 1404 Because during the Hundred Years War the French fleet attacked twice, the castle was built at the river mouth.

1580–1643 Sir Walter Raleigh and other sailors of his time used the port to bring back plundered cargo from Spanish treasure ships.

1620 *Mayflower* and *Speedwell* set sail from Bayards Cove only to return to Plymouth some 300 miles out for repairs. Following repairs the *Mayflower* set sail again and accomplished the crossing to America.

1643–46 During the English Civil War, Dartmouth fought for the Parliament. For four weeks it resisted the Royalist Prince Maurice and was recaptured three years later by Fairfax. Traces of a Civil War encampment can be found above Dartmouth Castle (Gallant's Bower).

1663–1729 Thomas Newcomen, inventor of the steam-driven piston for pumping out water from mines, was born in Dartmouth. An example of his steam engines can be seen next to the Tourist Information Centre.

1700–1800 Trading in clothing, ironware, wines and luxuries, Dartmouth became very wealthy. Trade was with Newfoundland, Spain, Portugal and Italy.

1900 Dartmouth lost its commercial importance, reverting to a coaling station supplying coal to the steam ships in the area and becoming a yachtsman's pleasure port.

1944 During the Second World War the Americans constructed approximately 480 landing craft for the landings on the Normandy beaches.

Left:
The naval College under construction 1904/5.
HMS Britannia *was used as one of the training ships until the College was completed. Also shown are the jetty and overhead gantry at Sandquay used for building materials.*

THE SOUTH HAMS
OF
Southern Devon

*Beesands Village
Fisherwomen 1898*

*In a Devonshire lane, as I trotted along
T'other day, much in want of a subject of song,
Thinks I to myself, I have hit on a strain,
Sure marriage is much like a Devonshire lane.*

*In the first place 'tis long, and when you are in it,
It holds you as fast as a cage does a linnet;
For however rough and dirty the road may be found,
Drive forward you must, there is no turning round.*

*Then long be the journey, and narrow the way
I'll rejoice that I've seldom a turnpike to pay:
And whatever others say, be the last to complain,
Though marriage is just like a Devonshire lane.*

Devonshire lanes and marriage seem unlikly bedfellows, but the Reverend Marriott's comparison is surely as valid today as when he wrote it a century ago.

In the county of Devon, the South Hams region is the most charming, varied and least spoiled by such tourist attractions as theme parks and rides. It still has the feel of tranquillity and freedom from everyday hassle; it travels at its own pace. The South Hams is very much an agricultural area with fertile soil that produces potatoes, cauliflower, cabbages and hot house fruit. The fishing industry, once a thriving activity, has decreased to a small number of ports, one of which is Dartmouth.

Dartmouth

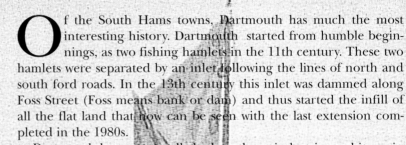

O f the South Hams towns, Dartmouth has much the most interesting history. Dartmouth started from humble beginnings, as two fishing hamlets in the 11th century. These two hamlets were separated by an inlet following the lines of north and south ford roads. In the 13th century this inlet was dammed along Foss Street (Foss means bank or dam) and thus started the infill of all the flat land that now can be seen with the last extension completed in the 1980s.

Dartmouth has never really had any large industries and its main wealth today comes from tourism and the Royal Naval College.

The College was first established in two wooden hulled Men-Of-War, *Britannia*, 1863, and the *Hindustan*, 1864, anchored in the estuary off Sandquay. The main building as we see it

The overhanging first floor of the Butterwalk (Duke Street), built between 1635 and 1640, sheltered traders underneath selling dairy products.

At that time it was possible to sail up to the rear of these buildings. Today the Butterwalk houses the town's Museum, which holds many interesting artefacts of bygone Dartmouth, including models and pictures of ships which came in to the port.

Some fine plaster moulding can be seen upstairs in the coffee shop next door. Fairfax Place is named after the English Civil War Parliamentarian, General Sir Thomas Fairfax (1612–71). No. 1 is a fine example of a seventeenth-century timber framed house still complete with original carved corner posts and window frames.

The Lower and Higher Ferries take passengers and cars across the river Dart. Higher Ferry started in 1825, driven by steam-powered draw chains, but was later replaced by more reliable horse power. Today both Ferries are motor driven and in the summer months Higher Ferry can get busy and passengers may expect to wait an hour or longer.

The Henly Museum, which includes a collection of Victorian artefacts in Anzac Street is worth a visit.

Above:
The Castle Hotel and Duke Street by the Quay c.1890, before the land beside the Butterwalk was infilled.

Left:
The old horseferry, crossing from Dartmouth to Kingswear, c.1890. It is known as the Lower Ferry.

Above:
The East Gate, rebuilt in 1990 after a fire, was once part of the town's fortifications.
Below:
Totnes bridge built in 1928, the last bridge to cross the River Dart.

The known beginnings of Totnes are in the 10th century, but according to legend Totnes is where the British people first began. The story goes that a young Trojan Prince, Brutus, with some followers left over from the wars with Greece in 1170BC set out in search of an island that Diana, Goddess of Love, had told Brutus would be his. Set in the pavement next to 51 Fore Street is the Brutus Stone. This is the first stone Brutus set foot on when landing in Britain which made him exclaim 'Here I stand and here I rest And this town shall be called Totnes'. Totnes (fort or lookout on a ridge of land) was a known fortified Saxon town built to guard the head of the river from marauding Vikings. It was a trading centre which minted its own coins. After the defeat of Harold in 1066 Totnes was given to Knight Judhel; he was instrumental in building the castle. The

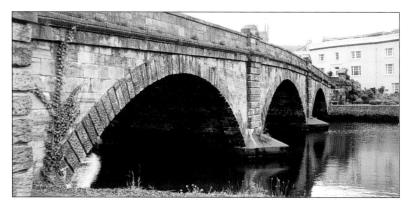

trading grew with France and along the coast with tin, slate, wool, cloth and products from the field. In the 16th century it was one of the top twenty richest towns in the country. As with Dartmouth it lost its importance in the 18th and 19th centuries. Now it relies on tourism and farming for its wealth.

The family of Charles Babbage, mathematician and inventor of the computer, came from Totnes and he studied at the local grammar school.There is a room in the local museum devoted to him.

William John Wills, son of a Totnes doctor, crossed Australia from south to north, to carry out surveying work to chart an inland route, but he died on the return trip. There is an obelisk near the bridge which commemorates this tragic event.

The town mill shows the development of Totnes over 1000 years from the Saxon settlement to the 19th century. The Tourist Information Centre is housed here.

The Elizabethan Museum (Fore Street), in a house built in 1575 for a rich cloth merchant, has fine examples of period furniture and costumes. A guessing game of unusual items held in the museum can puzzle children and adults for hours.

Above:
Parts of the Butterwalk are dated 1628 where shaded locations were used for selling dairy products.
Below:
Town Mill houses the TIC, dated 1588. The ground floor still keeps the layout of the old mill, while upstairs the past 1000 years of the town are documented.

Above:

The main entrance to the medieval town is shown here – before the clock was installed c.1880. Thought to date back to the 13th century it has undergone various changes over the years, the most notable being the removal of a smaller arch which was used for pedestrians, and extension of the cart arch to the size it is today.

Totnes Guildhall has a public gallery showing exhibits on Cromwell and the Civil War, and William J. Wills's expedition.

The Butterwalk's overhanging first floor rooms protect the traders from inclement weather.

Daniel Defoe (author of *Robinson Crusoe* and *Moll Flanders*) a merchant and great traveller in England visited Totnes between 1724 and 1726 and wrote:

About 22 miles from Exeter we go to Totnes on the river Dart. This is a very good town; of some trade, but has more gentlemen in it than tradesmen of note; they have a very fine stone–bridge here over the river, which being within seven or eight miles of the sea, is very large, and the tide flows 10 or 12 foot at the bridge. Here was had the diversion of seeing them catch fish, with the assistance of a dog. The case is this, on the south side of the river, and on a slip, or narrow cut or channel made for the purpose for a mill, there stands a corn–mill; the mill tail, or floor for the water below the wheels is wharfed up on either side with stone, above high–water mark, and for above 20 or 30 foot in length below it, on that part of the river towards the sea; at the end of this wharfing is a grating of wood, the cross–bar of which stand bearing inward, sharp at the end, and pointing inward towards one other, as the wires of a mouse trap.

When the tide flows up, the fish can with ease go in between the points of these cross–bars, but the mill being shut down they can go no further upwards; and when the water ebbs again, they are left behind, not being able to pass the points of the grating, outwards; which like a mouse–trap keeps them in, so that they are left at the bottom with about a foot, or a foot and a half water. We were carried hither at low water, where was saw about 50 or 60 small salmon, about 17 to 20 inches long, which the country people call salmon peal, and to catch these, the person who went with us, who was our landlord at a great inn next the bridge, put in a net on a hoop, which we call in this country a shove net: the net being fixed at one end of the place they put in a dog, who was taught his trade before hand, at the other end of the place, and he drives all the fish into the net, so that only holding the net still in its place, the man took up two or three and thirty salmon peal at the first time.

Below:

Train lines you can see in the forefront of the picture were used for transporting amongst other things timber, wine and cider from the warehouses along the river front, to the railway station.

The wagons were pulled by horses.

The picture also shows a busy market day.

BIGBURY BAY

The inset pictures show Inner Hope today and c. 1892.

There is a fine walk from here to the fort at Bolt Head.

Burgh Island, opposite Bigbury-on-sea, at the northern end of Bigbury Bay, south of Modbury on the B3392, accessible on foot at low tide, has a long history. A monastic order established itself there in AD900 but today all that remains of civilization is a pub and a hotel (which is probably all that's needed).

The hotel has had some famous visitors including Noel Coward, the King who abdicated for love (Edward VIII) and Mrs Simpson, and Agatha Christie, who wrote *Ten Little Nigger Boys* and *Evil Under the Sun* there.

During high tide the Island is cut off but a sea tractor operates to carry those who must.

Bigbury-on-sea has a large sandy beach and essential facilities.

Further south in Bigbury Bay and accessible from Bigbury-on-sea by travelling inland around the estuary and back again to the coast, lies Thurlestone, with its natural arch rock formation on the foreshore, and reputation as a smuggling village.

Travelling inland and out again Hope Cove, with its delightful small village, shop and pubs, can be reached by road. A Spanish galleon sank here after the Spanish Armada in 1588.

Above:
*Galpin Street, Modbury.
The town was part of
Kingsbridge, but this
was only a legal
link. The two towns
nearly came to blows
over the route of the new
rail link, but this was
overcome when it was
finally located far to the
north of Modbury.*

The Saxon meaning of Modbury is 'Moot Burgh' or meeting place. Records have been traced back to the 8th century. The eight-day fair, held in May, dates back to the 14th century.

The Exeter Inn in Church Street was the meeting place for the Royalists in the Civil War. Two battles were fought at Modbury, in 1642 and 1643. Plymouth was besieged by the Royalists. Parliament (Oliver Cromwell) raised a force of approximately 8000 men, some of whom had been marched down from the North to relieve them. The Royalists sent Sir Nicholas Slanning and Col. John Trevanion with a force of approximately 2000 men to Modbury to hold them back, and on 21 February these two forces met. As the Parliament forces were greater they drove the Royalists through the streets. They retreated to the fortified court house, which they held until the early morning of the following day, when they were forced to retreat again, along a street behind the Church, which is still known as Runaway Lane. The implication of this victory by the Parliamentary forces was the raising of the siege at Plymouth.

Modbury in the 19th century prospered from the wool industry and as a market town, but with the Industrial Revolution the cottage crafts of the woollen trade declined. Today Modbury is a small pleasant country town with other crafts to show, as in the fine examples of woodturning in the craft centre in New Street Crafts Centre. Old Mother Hubbard's house, a thatched 16th century property, now a restaurant, can be found on the A379 in Yealmpton.

SALCOMBE

alcombe like Dartmouth is best seen on foot. There are a couple of car parks only a short distance from the town centre, which is easily blocked with cars. A picturesque place, which has good restaurants, antique shops, craft shops featuring local artists, and several pubs, Salcombe is a town for gentle beach holidays, walking, lunching and relaxing.

There are several interesting historical features in Salcombe's past, one of which is given prominence in the Maritime and Local History Museum, near to the Post Office. This is especialy interesting for children, with features on knots, flags and finds from wrecks

in the area. In the 17th century pirates would anchor their boats in the estuary, come ashore, and rob the local farmers of their sheep and the townfolk of their fishing boats and anything else they could lay their hands on. This came to a head in 1625 when the fortified mansion of Sir William Courtenay at Ilton was attacked. Plates and other household goods were stolen. Forces were sent into the area to clear up the rabble. Records show a sum of £6 being spent to send these pirates to gaol.

Fort Charles just south of the town was rebuilt in 1643/4; it saw action in the English Civil War when the Royalists under Sir Edmund Fortescue with some 64 men, 8 guns and 2 washer women were laid siege to for four months by the Parliamentarian, Colonel Weldon. On the 7 May 1646 Sir Edmund agreed to surrender, as larger guns were brought in from Plymouth. After the siege Salcombe Castle was demolished to its present condition on the orders of the House of Commons.

Until the 19th century Salcombe's main business was ship building and in 1856 it only had two pubs of little stature and the shores around were almost unknown.

In the Second World War thousands of Americans GIs set sail in June 1944 for the D–Day landings in Normandy.

Left:
Salcombe boatyards c.1900. Salcombe grew quickly from a small fishing village. It has always had a better and bigger fishing fleet and shipbuilding facilities than Kingsbridge.

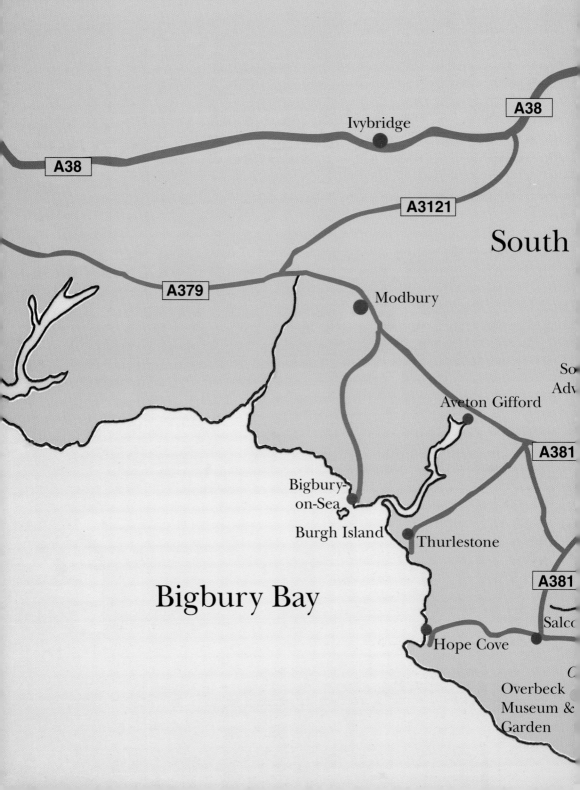

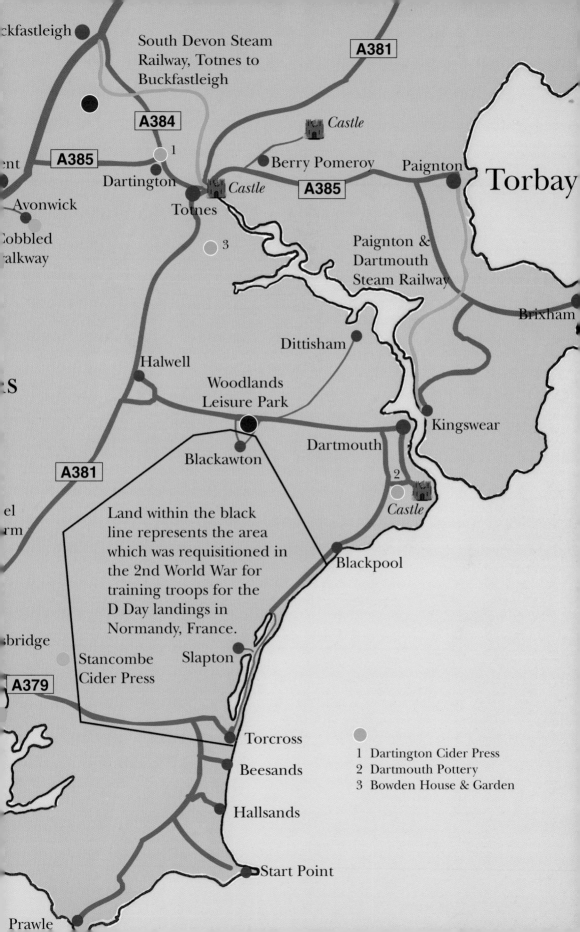

Buckfastleigh

South Devon Steam
Railway, Totnes to
Buckfastleigh

A381

A384

Castle

1

A385

Dartington

Berry Pomeroy

Paignton

A385

Avonwick

Castle

Totnes

Torbay

Cobbled
alkway

3

Paignton &
Dartmouth
Steam Railway

Brixham

Dittisham

Halwell

Woodlands
Leisure Park

Kingswear

A381

Blackawton

Dartmouth

el
rm

2

Castle

Land within the black
line represents the area
which was requisitioned in
the 2nd World War for
training troops for the
D Day landings in
Normandy, France.

Blackpool

sbridge

Stancombe
Cider Press

Slapton

A379

Torcross

1 Dartington Cider Press
2 Dartmouth Pottery
3 Bowden House & Garden

Beesands

Hallsands

Start Point

Prawle

Above:

Kingsbridge Market Place 1894 showing the Butterwalk and the town clock.

Above:

The town clock has only 3 faces, the fourth is blank, because it faced the workhouse.

Kingsbridge claims to be the capital of the South Hams. The estuary flows to its door steps and it is a town still blessed with small traders and small shops. The location of the bridge in its name has long been lost, and we are uncertain which king used it. Kingsbridge looks well after dark when its shops along its narrow streets are all lit up.

The records show that the Abbot of Buckfast let his monks set up an open air market in 1219. From the 14th to 19th century it was a well renowned port, shipping wool and sharp tools from local mills and foundries. It also had flour, cider, textile and brewing industries, but all these have gone.

St Edmunds Church built by the monks in the 15th century has an unusual epitaph inside the chancel door:

> *Robert Bone Phillip Buried 1793*
> *Here lie I at the chancel door.*
> *Here lie I because I'm poor,*
> *The further in the more you'll pay*
> *Here lie I as warm as they.*

The old Grammar School, built in 1670, is now The Cookworthy Museum; the boys carved their names on their desks even in the 17th century . The museum is named after William Cookworthy, who was born in Kingsbridge in 1705. He was the first person to make Cornish china clay into English porcelain. He discovered that when he fired moulded items of clay to above $1,000\,^{\circ}C$ they became a tough, vitreous material, cool white in colour and translucent when thin. (China clay porcelain was first produced in China in the 8th century.) This museum underwent a major refurbishment in 1998.

Other interesting items include the Shambles, whose stone pillars are over four hundred years old and are holding up the ceiling of the restaurant at the top of the town. The Kings Arms is an old coaching inn (1775) complete with archway. It used to take five days to travel from London to Kingsbridge.

The Tourist Information Centre is situated in the car park next to the estuary.

Above:
Kingsbridge Workhouse c.1837. This workhouse was built to take all the poor, sick, and insane from the South Hams area. But bringing them to a single building caused great sorrow,and it was a place to keep away from.

Left:
Quay garage c.1920 showing the estuary before it was filled in by the Salcombe road.

START BAY Torcross, Slapton Ley, Start Point

Above:
A Sherman Tank that was recovered from Start Bay now resides in Torcross car park.

Right:
Torcross today, with Slapton Ley behind the houses.

Above:
The base of the pill box acts as the outflow for the fresh water lake Slapton Ley.

Above:
Start Point Lighthouse. Built in 1834, its light has a reach of over 21 miles.

Right:
Torcross in c. 1890.

Torcross, Beesands, Hallsands, Blackpool, and Start Point all lie within Start Bay. At Beesands at certain times of the day you can buy locally caught fish from the fishermen. Torcross has changed very little over the years and still retains its shops and pubs. Slapton Ley is a freshwater lake divided from the sea by a shingle bank. The water flows into the sea behind the Torcross Hotel. At Start Point car park there is a fine walk down to the automatic lighthouse with views over Start Bay. Various sea birds can be seen sitting on the rocks. Looking out to sea you can see the earth's curve and imagine harsher times; in 1581 a pirate was hanged in chains here, as a warning to others.

The map on the centre page shows the area evacuated in Dec. 1943 to become a training area for the US 4th Division assault force for the D–Day landings in Normandy, France. The 3000 inhabitants were given just six weeks to move out all movable possessions. Apart from the buildings nothing was to be left. The area was chosen because it had the same terrain as the Utah landing beach. Unfortunately during one of the manoeuvers, German E boats attacked the landing craft and 749 Americans lost their lives. A Sherman Tank and Obelisk memorial have been erected to remember this tragedy.

Hallsands was once a thriving community of approximately 128 inhabitants making their living from the sea. The village was perched hard against the cliff face with a single road running through the middle. Protection from the forces of the sea was afforded by a large pebbled beach. Crabbing and fishing were the main activities, with the best of the catch being transported to London via Kingsbridge on the train. In April 1897 a contract was let to dredge 650,000 tons of gravel off the shore line of Start Bay, to extend Plymouth dock-yards. Once this was completed, by January 1902 the protection it afforded Hallsands was lost. The following storms in 1903/4 started undermining the rock face that the houses were built on. Then on 26 January 1917 came the end of the village. With a gale blowing fron the north–east and a high tide 27 houses collapsed and were washed into the sea. There is very little to see today apart from the roofs of two houses. The cliff is still eroding; it is not possible to pass any further than the cliff top.

Above:
Beesands today looking towards Start Point lighthouse.

Above:
Hallsands today.
You cannot proceed beyond this point as the cliff face is collapsing.

Left:
Blackpool Sands, an Award-winning family beach on the A379 between Dartmouth and Torcross.

Dartmouth Castle is signposted off the B3205 Dartmouth to Stoke Fleming road. The castle we see today was first started in 1481 and its sister fort on the Kingswear side was built between 1491 and 1502. But of an earlier castle, first referred to in 1388, the wall above the car parking area is a prominent part. The present church dates back to 1641, but mention is made of an earlier church in 1192. The castles had a metal chain drawn between them called Old Jaw Bones to stop any ships travelling further into the port. The castle at Dartmouth was one of the first to be built for artillery. A newer Victorian coastal defence battery next to the castle shows a fine set of cannon and ammunition-holding areas. The castle is situated on an outcrop of stone at the edge of the bay with a fine view looking out to sea. There is a grass bank for picnics and a small cafeteria. The parking is very limited.

Right:
Bayards Castle overlooks the narrowest point of the inlet but being close to the water level and small gun port apertures it has a limited field of fire. It was used in 1940 as a machine gun post. Free entry, open daily.

Totnes Castle is situated in the town. The castle you see today was rebuilt in the 1320s by the De la Zouche family which had replaced a wooden castle built by Breton, Judhael. It is a fine example of a motte and bailey castle. From the top there is a magnificent view. The huge earth mound is of Norman descent. In the 15th century the castle fell into disrepair. The castle took no major part in the Civil War. It was taken over by the state in 1947.

Above:
Totnes Castle 1904.

Left:
The North Gate, c.1845. The Totnes town wall was built around AD907 with three gates. It encompassed all the buildings, but by the 1600s just the three gates stood, with new buildings being built outside the East and West Gates. By then the fortification which the wall offered was no longer required.

Above:
*Berry Pomeroy Castle
gatehouse.*

*The Castle from
Gatcombe Brook.*

Berry Pomeroy Castle is signposted off the A385 from Totnes to Paignton. It was built in the late 15th century in an unusual location for a castle; on a wooded rocky outcrop above Gatcombe Park. The mansion and fortifications are in ruin but you can still see the splendour and craftsmanship of the work. There is a grassed area at the side of the castle for picnics with a small cafeteria open in the summer months. The castle was built for the Pomeroy family who first came to Devon with William the Conqueror. Its defences were built for attack by small-scale marauders only. A large scale attack could not properly be withstood. (The Pomeroys came from a small French village near Falaise in Normandy.)

The castle stayed in the hands of the Pomeroys until 1549 when it was bought by the Seymours who in 1600 undertook a grand works programme to extend the property. But financial difficulties prevented the work from being completed, as can be seen today in the unfinished external walls. It stayed in the family until the 1930s, when it reverted to

Toothing stones project from the kitchen block, awaiting the new west wing which was never started.

the state. There is very little indication of how the castle fell into ruin.

In 1688 William of Orange, on his way from Brixham to become King, stayed at the castle, but in 1701 John Prince the local vicar wrote 'All this glory lieth in dust, buried in its own ruines'. The castle is said to be the most haunted in Britain. Some visitors have claimed to have seen a ghost of a 'Blue Lady'. One of the Pomeroy family, she was reputed to have had a baby by her father and then strangled it. Some visitors have reported suddenly feeling cold and others have found strange figures appearing on pictures they have taken at the castle. The castle is open between March and October.

Right:
Inner courtyard dating from 1590. The Castle consists of two parts. The guardroom and ramparts are 14th century, and the Mansion 16th century. The stone used by the Pomeroys was slate from a local quarry, but the Seymours used local stone from the valley floor.

Below:
Cider was once a very important trade, with major sea-borne export value. It was said in 1808 that every valley in the South Hams is occupied with orchards, which are much celebrated for the excellence of the cider they produce.
Symons from Totnes claimed they made the finest cider. They were large employers of labour and offered prizes for the best kept orchards.

Overbeck Museum & Garden. From Malborough on the A381 past Kingsbridge take a right hand turn to Combe and it is signposted from there. The 6-acre gardens contain a fine selection of plants seldom found in this country, with views overlooking Salcombe estuary. The house holds many interesting items from birds' eggs, butterflies, man–traps to dolls houses and dolls. Gardens open all the year, house April–October. (NATIONAL TRUST)

Bowden House, and Museum. Leave Totnes on the A381 towards Halwell and signposted to your left is Ashprington. Bowden House is part Tudor and part Queen Anne, with tales of the unexplained ghost sightings. The photographic Museum has a display of black and white prints showing past times, with a 77-seater cinema showing oldie films. Open April to October. Café/Shop.

Dartington Cider Press Centre. Situated on the A384 out of Dartington, this former cider-making complex has been converted into shops selling quality items made from glass, wood, silver and ceramics. Good wholesome country cooking is also available.

Dartmouth Pottery. Open all year. Situated on the B3205 Dartmouth to Stoke Fleming road, famous for its gulping fish and pottery classic cars. Open all year. (Seconds Shop)

Kingsbridge to Salcombe ferry trips boats depart from Kingsbridge Quay and ferry boat yard and the Ferry Inn steps at Salcombe.

River Dart Cruises from Dartmouth to Totnes 1hr or 1.5hr trips, coastal cruises or 200hp powerboat trips to the Mew stone at the entrance to Dartmouth harbour to see grey seals, kittiwake, cormorant and other coastal birds; all these trips can be booked at kiosks along Dartmouth Marina.

Stancombe Cider, situated above Sherford on the A379 between Kingsbridge and Torcross. The cider is made on site by the 300 year-old press from locally-grown cider apples. (Free samples)

Lunches and cream teas served in the restaurant; access via single track and roads with passing places. Watch the cows being milked. Open April–October, plus other days.

Dartington Hall Leaving Dartington on the A384 Dartington Hall can be found by taking the first right hand turning before the church. Gardens can be visited.

Kingsbridge Cookworthy Museum After a major refurbishment in 1998, this museum in the old school takes you back to the Kingsbridge of the past. You can still see where the boys carved their names in the desks.

Totnes Elizabethan Museum This museum in a large Elizabethan merchant's town house, has lots of interesting things to see, and a guessing game for children.

Shipwrecks:
Prawle Point, at least 8 ships have sunk here. One was a Dutch East Indian named 'De Boot' (The Ship) in 1738 carrying diamonds; local people from East Prawle helped to take the boxes ashore, but not all were accounted for. The San Pedro El Mayor (St Peter the Great) a ship of the Spanish Armada crashed into the rocks at Hope Cove in November 1588. Most of the crew got away and were imprisoned in a local barn. A Spanish helmet of the time can be seen at the Cookworthy Museum.

Left:
Salcombe Lifeboat from 1887–1904. The lifeboat house still can be seen today next to the South Sands Hotel. Another building for the same purpose can be seen at Inner Hope. This station closed in 1930.

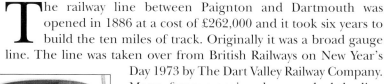

Above:
Kingswear Station
coaches awaiting their
passengers.

The railway line between Paignton and Dartmouth was opened in 1886 at a cost of £262,000 and it took six years to build the ten miles of track. Originally it was a broad gauge line. The line was taken over from British Railways on New Year's Day 1973 by The Dart Valley Railway Company. Many famous engines have worked the line including the *Flying Scotsman* in September 1973. The line was initially intended to cross the River Dart near the Higher Ferry, Dartmouth, but the landowner of the time had other ideas and the line was constructed as you see it today.

The ride is one of the most delightful short railway journeys you can take. Passengers who move from side to side of the carriage will see the coastal views at Torbay. Then after emerging from Greenway Tunnel the estuary of the Dart.

Left:
Engine 4588 at Paignton Station. The track
gradients of 1 in 66–75 suit this type of engine.

SOUTH DEVON RAILWAY

The South Devon Railway runs between Buckfastleigh and Totnes for approximately 7 miles alongside the river Dart. The scenery is some of the most beautiful in Devon. At Buck-fastleigh there is a small museum, showing the history of the line with exhibits including the only surviving broad gauge locomotive from Brunel's time.

The railway line between South Brent and Kingsbridge was opened in 1893 at a cost of £180,000. There were four stations – Avonwick (which has been converted into a private house), Gara Bridge, Loddiswell and Kingsbridge. The line was approximately 12 miles long, had 48 wrought-iron bridges and a 640 yard tunnel which can still be seen today at Sorley Tunnel Adventure Farm. It was called the Primrose Line because in the springtime the track side was a carpet of primroses. The line was closed in the 1960s.

Above:
Train arriving at
Staverton Station.

Right:
Sorley Tunnel today. You can walk down the
embankment and into the tunnel.

For the Children

Below:
The Herzogin Cecilie, *built in Germany in 1902, was a famous record breaking clipper ship capable of 20 knots. In 1936, she was carrying grain to Ipswich when she hit the Ham Stone. She was towed to Starhole Bay, just south of Salcombe where she sunk. Today you can look down from the path above the Bay and see the dark shape underwater.*

Pennywell Farm. Situated off the A38 between Buckfastleigh and the A385 junction to Totnes, Pennywell is an adventure farm with pigs, cows, sheep, goats, and a pony. Activities include a Commando Course, basket-making, stencilling, bottle feeding young animals, collecting eggs, and every half an hour there is a new farm activity or event. Open April to October.

Woodlands, A Leisure Park situated near Blackawton, signposted off the A3122 between Dartmouth and Halwell. Woodlands offers Calippo Canyon twisty water courses, a Toboggan run, Bumper boats, Indoor Venture Zones, Falconry Centre, and various animals, birds and entertainments. Cafeteria open daily.

Sorley Tunnel, Adventure Farm. Signposted off the A381 above Kingsbridge, just after Churchstow heading towards Halwell. Sorley Tunnel is a 200-acre organic working dairy farm with side attractions of Pirate Playslide, peddle carts, trampolines, and Adventure Zone, the 640-yard railway tunnel, and woodland walks.

At Avonwick there is a rare example of a cobbled stone track of some 200 metres which was probably used for the transport of slate from the quarries at Diptford to South Brent. The cobbles have been re-laid in some areas and in others you can still see the ruts made by the heavy wagons. The river Avon flows along one side whilst the old redundant Primrose Line is on the other. There is a small parking area next to the two bridges and the old toll house opposite the turning to Diptford.

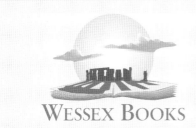

WESSEX BOOKS

Other titles by
WESSEX BOOKS include:
• ARTHUR Land and Legend
• WESSEX A Journey through 2000 years
• LEYLINES of Wessex
• CROP CIRCLES of Wessex
• CHALK FIGURES of Wessex
• THOMAS HARDY of Wessex
• A Taste of YORKSHIRE
• SIR CHRISTOPHER WREN

Wessex Books, 2 Station Cottages,
Newton Toney, Salisbury,
Wiltshire SP4 0HD
Telephone 01980 629349
Facsimile 01980 629349

Acknowledgements

For the use of photographs the publishers gratefully thank:

The Cookworthy Museum Photographic Collection, pp. ii, 1, 11 inset, 12, 13 bottom, 16 top, 17, 18 bottom left and right, 25, 28;
Dartmouth Museum, pp. 4, 5;
J.L. Harvey, p. ii inset;
Greg Norden, p. 2;
The Totnes Museum Photographic Collection, pp. 7 bottom left, 8, 9, 21, 24.

Cover illustration by Matthew Harvey.

Published by Wessex Books 1999.
Text © Robert Drake.
Design © Wessex Books 1999.

Printed in Great Britain by
Brunton Business Publications Ltd.

ISBN 0 9529619 9 7

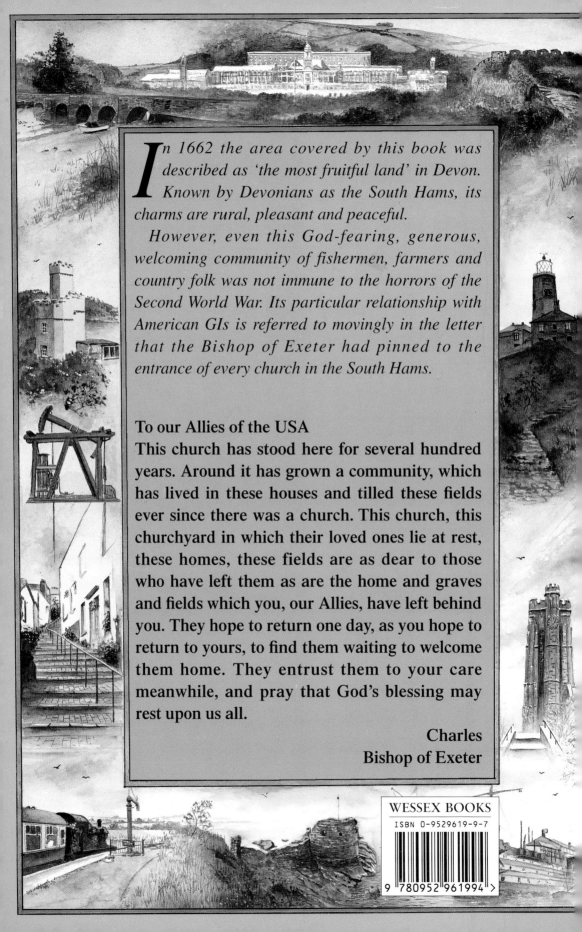

In 1662 the area covered by this book was described as 'the most fruitful land' in Devon. Known by Devonians as the South Hams, its charms are rural, pleasant and peaceful.

However, even this God-fearing, generous, welcoming community of fishermen, farmers and country folk was not immune to the horrors of the Second World War. Its particular relationship with American GIs is referred to movingly in the letter that the Bishop of Exeter had pinned to the entrance of every church in the South Hams.

To our Allies of the USA
This church has stood here for several hundred years. Around it has grown a community, which has lived in these houses and tilled these fields ever since there was a church. This church, this churchyard in which their loved ones lie at rest, these homes, these fields are as dear to those who have left them as are the home and graves and fields which you, our Allies, have left behind you. They hope to return one day, as you hope to return to yours, to find them waiting to welcome them home. They entrust them to your care meanwhile, and pray that God's blessing may rest upon us all.

Charles
Bishop of Exeter

WESSEX BOOKS
ISBN 0-9529619-9-7

9 780952 961994